In Transit

In Transit
Love Poems to the City

Clare Morris

Angela Center Press
Santa Rosa, California
www.angelacenter.com

Library of Congress Control Number 2005934920

Front cover and inside photos: Ted Sexauer
Back cover photo: Donna Hardy
Cover Design: Nancy Brink
Book Design: Anne Richardson-Daniel

Excerpt from *Lastingness*
Czeslaw Milosz, New and Collected Poems (1931 – 2001)
by permission, Harper Collins Publishers, Inc. © 2001

In Gratitude

For Donna Hardy, long-time friend, writer, teacher, and mentor to me; for Nancy Sue Brink, poet and filmmaker, of Present-Tense Productions in Redwood City, California, for her artful editorial support; for Ted Sexauer and his imaginative photographs; for Maureen Adams, Joyce Brady, Fred Marchant and Gene Sandretto, who early-on read the manuscript and affirmed my vision for this book; for Ron Jones, San Francisco writer and performer, whose regard for cities helped to inspire my own; for Angela Center Press, whose encouragement made this book possible; and for Intentional Productions of Pasadena who formed it all into a book.

Dedication

To you whose names I do not know
whom I have met on buses,
streets and other city spaces.
You have been my teachers.

That was in a big city, no matter what country, what
    language,
A long time ago (blessed be the gift
Of spinning a tale out of a trifle,
In the street, in a car – I write it down not to lose it).

                    – Czeslaw Milosz from *Lastingness*

My City, My Self

Cities are filled with caterpillars. I met one on a bone-chilling November day in San Francisco. Laden with packages and lost in thought, I climbed the Divisadero Street hill, between Sacramento and Clay. A boy, about seven, danced up the sidewalk ahead of me, skipping and twirling to his own music. As my long legs caught up with him, we spoke.

> "It's cold today – too cold for butterflies," he said.
> "You're right," I nodded.
> "They won't last through winter."
> "No."
> "I collect them. Black and red and white ones are
>   my favorites. But they're gone now."
> "They're asleep till spring," I suggested.
> "They don't sleep. They die. And then they come
>   back as butterflies," he insisted.

This child knew his caterpillar nature. He understood something of death and rebirth. We met in the wonder of a mystery common to both of us, a mystery rooted in the ways of earth.

Cities are indeed filled with caterpillars – their chrysalis pods and what takes wing from them in the fullness of time. Cities are fields of transformation, cauldrons of conflict, gardens of herbs poisonous and healing. They are hives of industry, as well as desiccated wastelands. They are looms of converging human threads, weaving differences of culture and paradigm into shifting, vulnerable fabrics. They are vast theaters for the one drama of creation, in which we, the players, enact the variations.

We can put our arms around this totality in a city as small and compact as San Francisco. With seawater on three sides, San Francisco recalls the walled cities of medieval times. The City by the Bay is a knowable, walkable reality, reminding us that we can also know something of our inner population, history and geography. When we contemplate a city like San Francisco – discovering its seaside charm, love for the arts, and ethnic diversity, its homelessness, poverty, and gang warfare – we also contemplate ourselves. We, too, carry these qualities and capacities within. Each of us is an entire city, which we will never finish exploring.

On Divisadero Street that November morning, I did not realize what a mirror the city holds out to us. We make of the world "a replica of our unknown face," wrote Carl Jung. This ability to look into ourselves, as we look into the world around us, is a way of learning, that we might know the value and uniqueness of who we are.

When we enter into a city with awareness, we participate in what is alive in all that we experience. Each of these happenings can be understood as chrysalis events, which will hatch in us, when the time for butterflies is ripe.

Contents

STOP REQUESTED

PLEASE HOLD ON

THANK YOU FOR RIDING MUNI

MEETING YOUR CITY

HOME

IMAGICIAN

Long ago I lived where vineyards, lambs
and freeways met. There I learned
to turn tire sounds into ocean surf
and honking into migrating geese.

Now I live in a city by the sea.

Pile drivers are talking drums.
Growling cars are tigers on the hunt.
Leaf blowers are swarming bees.
Buzz saws are hyenas.
Car alarms are exotic birds.
Sirens are coyotes.

ABSENCE

Early March was sunny and warm,
seducing us to open windows wide
and put away winter coats too soon.

Today cold rain chills the city,
seeps under snug doors, finds its way
up sleeves, down necks, through
shoelaces and soles –
                                    I miss

the shadows of sunlight
that send shutter slats across
wallpaper and family photographs.
I miss woven branch patterns
over benches and sidewalks. I miss
turning arcs of poles and ladders,
as they tilt into light
and trace the turning earth –
                                    I miss

the light source itself,
showering silent gold over every
grand home and cardboard shelter, every
limousine and grocery cart, every
smallest bit of being, beneath
its fiery fertile eye.

SMALLER THAN SMALL

Each day I hold a singing bowl
and strike it.
A genie of sound appears, circling
the room, healing the world.
One day, I strike the shining form,
and see inside a single strand of silk,
shaking with vibrations.
The tiny spinner of this bridge
clings to her thread, though the anchors
of her world prove unsteady.
She holds fast, riding the living sound
and disappears.

DIVA

I heard a mockingbird sing
grand opera last night,
ringing a clear bel canto
into warm summer dark,
seeding the hours,
where a dream unfolded
as a blue green turtle,
who crept from under
my golden pillow, and into my
open hand laid a lavender egg
that hatched a child singing
arias for the joy of being.

LITTLE BUT OH MY

Ants flow across my marble sink
in graceful swirling patterns. I watch them, awed
by how they risk giants' careless feet,
puppies' long inquisitive tongues,
and drowning in rain drops
as they climb three floors to my kitchen.

My admiration is boundless. I am
planning their poison. I make it
on my stove: sugar, water, boric acid.
Knowing I take life, I pour tiny pools of the brew
into the smallest of saucers. I wait and watch,
as they move toward their deadly drink.
I hear the dirge of their kinfolk rise high and higher,
as they come to retrieve the bodies.
I sing to them, and offer a garden cemetery.

ENERGY CRISIS

Coyote laughs
and laughs again,
plays with the hum
and sparkle of excess.
Twirling his tail,
he flickers, dims,
disconnects.
"For your own good,"
he chuckles and winks,
unplugging our lavish lives.
We are left in the cold dark,
shouldering close to each other
beneath brightening stars.

PATIENCE

For thirty years
I have regarded this artichoke,
dry and lovely in its death.

Long gone to seed,
its half dozen stalks stand
proud in a white vase.
Upon each stem sits
the plain head of a noble
flower, now a round field
of empty pods,
framed by a leafy corona.

Today I see a difference.
at the edge of the largest
flower, a single seed
has risen like a dandelion star.
Its long white hairs sway as they
barely touch the empty pods.
The impossible is poised,
ready for flight.

EARLY HOPE

Each late winter, Mother would clip
the first flowering quince and carry
the red blooms on their black stems
into the dining room,
where they could watch themselves unfold
in a mirror above her linen chest.

She never studied ikebana.
She knew it in her bones, and would gaze
at the blossoms, touching their impossibility,
then close her eyes and smile.
She never mentioned the storms
that would soon break upon the quince tree.
She didn't like dark thoughts.
Or dark dreams. Or winter.

ONLY THIS

a square of sunlight
fills an earthen bowl
raising bread loaves
as it passes

BEAUTY PASSING THROUGH

Morning sun through
plum trees and shutters
turns across an open threshold.

SEWING TIME

Pine needle wind
threading the hours.
Autumn tapestry.

LOVELY ABSENCE

Time and winter rain
jewel a maple's naked branch,
recalling red ghost leaves,
crimson October lifted
in winds of separation.

WIND FALL

It falls slowly into my lap,
a sycamore leaf, as though
today's July were October.
I hold the weightless body,
trace curves and gnarls
of fingers
and the secret center
deep in the bowl
of a twisted hand.
A bird takes flight, a ship
sails through bracing wind.
Fragile beauty, my life,
briefly green, its form soon
curling, released
by the living tree.

I lay the leaf down,
brown, in the dust.

JEREMIAH OUTSIDE MY GATE

A man neither young
nor old, wearing shirt
and slacks that beg
for sun, shuffles past,
clutching his chest,
lamenting
"Oh God — Oh God —
people are killing
all around, killing.
It isn't fair!"

I watch him weave
up the street, lean
on the mailbox, cross
Earth's meridians,
cry out on every continent
"Oh God —
            Oh!"

NIGHT VISION

Folded glasses
slipped into their case.
Magnifying lens
wrapped in velvet.
Contacts
shut in shallow wells.

Three layers for looking through
put away for the night,
that I might see clearly
into dark.

"After they'd gone, we noticed it."

ALLEY CABARET

They moved away, the neighbors across the street. After they'd gone, we noticed it.

In the alley next to the empty house, stood a round stool and an heirloom upright piano, its ivory keys chipped and grooved by decades of small children learning to play Für Elise and teenagers ripping through endless broken Chopsticks.

The family left on Saturday. The movers didn't return till Monday. The piano waited and begged for playmates.

Saturday afternoon, Mr. Robert Chan, home early from the bank, put down his monogrammed briefcase, mounted the piano stool and let his hands almost remember Chopin's Raindrop Prelude. He played it first like a shy lover.

Confidence grew, even longing — until three giggling boys ran by, ending his debut. He emerged walking slow, wiping his eyes, gazing at light on the laurel trees in front of his house.

Late that night, Bill Benson and Aida Conforti walked home from the movies. They heard Sid Farrell's cat run up and down the keys and hurried into the alley to have some fun. Bill sat on the stool, with Aida on his lap and round they went, till the top and the two of them came off spinning. Laughing, they put themselves and the stool together and played a duet: Swing Low, Sweet Chariot, then All Night, All Day, Someone's Watchin' Over Me,

My Lord, holding the whole neighborhood in the arms of a lullaby. No one threw shoes or shouted for them to stop.

At 8:00 Sunday morning, Barbara Ann Smiley reached the alley, carrying old Methodist hymnals, their pages fluttering after her as she walked. She settled on the stool as though she were in Carnegie Hall, and twirled herself to exactly the right height for her short, substantial legs and Sunday pumps. Smells of bacon and fresh coffee curled around her, as she gave her enthusiastic alto to The Old Rugged Cross, I Would Be True and For the Beauty of the Earth. She went through one book, skipped the ones she didn't like, moved into the second, and didn't rise from the stool for two hours. Abigail Selby, a morning walker, stopped to join in Just a Closer Walk With Thee, and Martha Kirkham, whose kitchen windows faced the alley, opened them wide so she could sing, too, while making cinnamon rolls.

On Monday morning, Mrs. Teresa Rodriguez whispered, "Ghosts!" to Keji, the mailman. "Someone played Scott Joplin every single hour last night. Whenever I leaned out my bedroom window to see who it was, no one was there — but the music continued!" "The piano must be haunted," he whispered.

About noon, the movers returned, their van open, empty and waiting for the old upright. When the door closed and the truck rolled out of sight, sunlight filled the alley.

IN TRANSIT

IN TRANSIT

When I climb onto the MUNI, I climb into the human condition. Who and what I find inside this wheeled box is never predictable and always intriguing. I find us there, myself there.

Looking out through bus windows – greasy or rained and steamed into impressionist paintings – I watch my city go by and muse on the micro-worlds of cars. Had I been able to drive, I, too, would be out there in traffic: warm, dry, air conditioned, conversing, learning French, singing out loud.

I ride public transportation instead. Here I find a micro-world of a different sort. It is vulnerable, inclusive, full of surprise, delight, and danger. Looking into any cluster of us riding together between stops offers a choice: go numb and think about something else, or pay attention and contemplate us.

If we choose to experience bus travel, we join an assortment of people who share brief journeys of transition. They represent a world of humans who continually meet and part, imprinting each other in ways that are haunting, painful, inspiring, and hilarious. These bus rides are short. So are our lives. We are always in transit, always moving, even in our stillness. The course of a bus route is a hologram of our fleeting travels alone-together on Planet Earth.

REFUGE

Rain falls over my city tonight.
Tiny lights from last December
edge an occasional eave. Headlights
shine through watery beams,
bright eyes needing to weep.

Traffic lights and neon come-ons
blink and stare at homeless wanderers.
Wearing black garbage bags, they crouch
behind shopping carts mountained
with sodden ruins, fragments of their years.

A bus approaches, the one I've been
waiting for. I step to a gutter streaming
with styrofoam and condoms.
I shake my umbrella before boarding,
spraying a galaxy of water sparks,
as though I were making the rain.

Inside the steaming canister,
lit by fluorescent tubes, I sit
next to a woman whose head
is wrapped in a damp white cloth
wound across the shoulders of a
full-length coat, quivering
with rain beads. She picks up
canvas bags of bread to make room.
We smile and look briefly
into each other's eyes.

WAITING FOR THE POLK 19

Restless, hot,
without hats or fog.
Necks craned north,
sorting through trucks, vans,
hunting for the Polk 19.
A twelve-year old boy, in shorts
and a Bob Marley tee shirt,
sees it first. The crowd cheers.

Round a corner,
rolls the bus,
looking tired as we are,
having to carry the weight
of us all.

HOSTESS
47 Van Ness, Monday, 5:00 p.m.

Packed body to body,
our hubbub hard-edged,
one voice rises above all others.
A slight, furtive woman clings
to a pole at the center door.
"Thank you for coming,"
she tells each rider
who squeezes out at a stop.
"I hope to see you again."

BEFORE SUNRISE
Balboa 31, 6:00 a.m., riding East

Going to work in the Avenues,
sleepy people doze, munch, sip
beneath signs in capital letters:
    NO FOOD OR DRINK
The bus brakes mid-block.
Doors fold open with a slap.
Shoes scrape in the dark.
Crutches thrust inside.
A wool-wrapped Asian man
pulls up the steps, coins in hand.
A woman with four tote bags
whispers to me,
"Driver has his own rules.
Stops here every day.
For him."

WHAT ENDURES
24 Divisadero, heading North, down Castro

He gets on at Castro and Eureka.
"Hey Tom — " a voice calls.
"Hey yourself, Michael."
"How's Bill?"
"Died. Last December."

"AIDS."
Passengers grow still.
"What now for you?"
"Working at Safeway.
He couldn't pay his debts.
I can.
Every minute I'm working
I feel close to him."

KIN

4 Sutter, Friday Afternoon

Two boys, age 10, wearing pop-singer t-shirts,
hair spiked by default, sit up front,
kick the wheel case with their tennies.
"Do you have brothers and sisters?" asks one.
"Oh yes. We have a blended family.
My half-sister, Amy, is also my first cousin,
and my step-brother, Tim, is really my nephew,
but he's older than me. How about you?"
The other boy squints, looks around, then down.
"I'm an only child."

INN OF THE GREYHOUND

Mother and child
edge down the aisle,
wrapped in crocheted wool,
tassels dancing.
In the young mother's mouth,
a pacifier.
Riders make room.
May the years be as kind.

LEGACY

7 Haight, going West. Noon.

He rants to the driver: "White kids,
rich kids, livin' on the backs of us.
Sissies. Soft. Don't know nothin'
'bout seein' family killed,
'bout bein' burned, buried alive."

He fills the sunlit bus with clouds
of grief that bring him to his feet,
turn him toward me. He walks
slowly, unsteadily, past
the empty seats, to where I sit.

I do not meet his eyes.
He stands over me.
The driver stops, opens the doors.
The man lurches out into a sea wind.
I breathe it, breathe it, breathe it.

DOING HER PART
7 Haight, toward Clayton

At Ashbury, she gets on.

Long gray hair swirls
around a peasant blouse,
tucked into a floor length
Indian bedspread skirt.
She's barefoot, carrying
only a broom.
The driver nods,
waves her past.

She doesn't sit down.
She sweeps:
under the first row,
out to the aisle,
under the second,
out to the aisle,
crossing, re-crossing
the ridged rubber mat,
making neat little piles
of dust and debris,
from one end
to the other:
"Cleanin' up this dump."

URBAN SUSPICION
5 Jackson, Evening Rush Hour

A man in tweeds,
expensive shoes,
sidles close
to a spectacled girl
who hangs on a strap
with one hand,
reads Bonjour Tristesse
with the other.
Sliding his fingers
into the clasp
of her swaying bag,
he digs deep inside.
"My feet!" she screams.
He slips away.
"You stomped on my feet!"
"I saw a man try to rob you,"
says an elderly woman,
"If I'd warned you out loud,"
no telling — ."

JUKE BOX BLUES
6 *Masonic, turning West on Clayton*

A middle-aged student climbs on
with bags, books, food for the day.
She drops coins in the fare box, smiles
as though Judy Garland might sing
Somewhere Over the Rainbow.

The driver turns sharply,
sending her backwards,
slamming against
folding front doors
that hold like a mother's arms,
steady as she falls.

The driver studies the street ahead.

OLD WARS

5 Fulton, September Afternoon

He must be eighty.
Sun in his face,
straw hat pulled low
over gray eyes adrift
in a wrinkled sea of white skin.
He hisses at a fit and cocky
African-American man,
"Get out of my way!"
"In your way? No way!
   Come on by."   "I said,
get out of my —"   "And I
said I'm not —"   "You people
are all in the way!"
The old man stumbles,
   backwards, a woman
thrusts herself between them,
is hit in the eye.
The driver says nothing,
looks straight ahead,
opens the doors.

TUTOR

6 Masonic, toward Parnassus. January.

Lilac in the air: loquacious woman
barely wearing a silver skirt,
pussy-cat stockings,
low-cut black sweater.
Next to her: girl with virginal face,
Peter Pan collar, plaid skirt,
lap full of school books.
Lilac lady: "Long night!
Real sore 'down there.'
Know what I mean?"
"Not really," blushes the girl,
"But it must feel awful."
"Thanks, hon —." Her eyes glisten.
"You wanna' know what else?"
Mascara spills down her left cheek.

WINDOW SHOPPING
Divisadero 24, North, down Castro

"I saw Johnny yesterday. What a hunk!"
"Remember, he's taken."
"I know. But just because I'm not buying
the meal, doesn't mean I can't look at
the menu."

REGULATIONS
1 California, riding through Chinatown

At the Powell stop, doors bump open.
Thirty people wait to squeeze inside.
An Asian woman climbs on first,
carrying groceries and a live chicken.
"Lady, you can't bring that bird on the bus."
"My dinner."
"Fine, but you can't get on with that chicken."
"My dinner."
"You have to get off — now."
He stands up.
She backs down the stairs.
She swings the chicken at a lamp post.
She's still first in line.
She climbs on again,
chicken limp over one arm.
"OK now?"

MILK
6 Masonic at Buena Vista Park

We see her from the bus windows,
student in her twenties, flying
down the Frederick Street hill,
loaded with books and a feedbag purse,
she tumbles, lands in a sprawl,
yards from the arriving bus.
Its doors open. It waits.
No one honks or yells at her to hurry.

She gathers herself, boards, hangs on a pole.
"May I hold your books?" asks a woman.
She fumbles for her fare, finds no wallet.
"Do you need bus fare?" asks a man.

Her transfer stop comes quickly.
She prepares to leave.
"Wait," says a teenage girl.
"I saw you'd left your wallet at home.
Do you have enough money for lunch?"

PRINCE
38 Geary

He sits shining
like a new-washed window
in a starched white shirt,
perfect Windsor knot
binding his neck
tight as King Tut's.

No books.
He grins, spine straight
in a graduation gown.
His robe confers
a kingly aura,
recalls unknown ancestors:
African chiefs, medicine men,
artists, ambassadors, inventors.

At Jefferson Junior High,
he rises from his front seat,
tall as the sky,
strides down the aisle,
alights from the back door.

Traffic stops.
He crosses the street.
The wind bends down
to pick up his hem
and carry his train,
billowing him to the curb
and years yet to be.

SILVER LINING
Geary 38, Saturday Afternoon

Like pack animals, riders shift and sigh,
burdened by bags lumpy with groceries,
gym shoes, and rented movies.
Outside, fog is a breaking wave
curling slow over its beach of sky
and Japantown.

The driver lets go with a song:
You are my sunshine,
my only sunshine.
You make me happy
when skies are gray —
he calls, "Sing with me!"

No one stirs.
"I dare you!"
Some smile,
others scowl.

"You in the pink blazer —
ever sing this song?
Sing it with me. I need company."
The chorus of riders joins his plea,
glad not to have been chosen.
"Ok," mumbles the blond in pink.

Next stop, Arguello," the driver calls,
and begins to sing:
You are my sunshine,
my only —
Sunshine. You make me happy —
girl in pink sings with him
— when skies are gray —
others join
You'll never know dear —
Arguello arrives
how much I love you —
doors open to applause
from the waiting crowd.

BUTTERFLY LESSON
80, Golden Gate Transit

No seats on the northbound bus, but one,
next to a sleepy child, about six,
lying across two spaces. I edge in,
steer little white tennies toward the floor.

The child sits up, fighting, confused,
calling in Spanish to her Mama
sitting behind us. Mama's looking down,
gaze fixed.

The child settles.
"Como se llama?" I ask
"Tanya," she whispers.
"Me llamo Clara," I tell her.
"Do you speak Spanish?" she asks.
"Mas o menos," I say.
"I don't understand Spanish," she shrugs.

"I'm ten," she tells me, "No — eight.
And I'm sick. My ear hurts. I can't hear good.
My stomach hurts. I can't breathe good."
I make small groans for her.

"My mama's mama has a mama
who has a mama, who has a mama," she says.
"Yes," I nod.
"It's true for all the people on this bus."
"Yes."

"Will they die when they get old?"
"Yes."
"Are you very old?" she asks.
"Not very old. Just old."
"Will you die?"
"Yes."

"I'll miss you. I'll be sad," she says.
"I'll miss you, too," I say,
not knowing what I mean.

We look at each other
without speaking.

Then I bat my eyes.
"How do you do that?" she asks.
"This way — up and down, up and down,
like a butterfly's wings."
She tries. Her lids won't obey.

"Let them flutter," I say.
She practices quietly,
looking out the window.

THE DIFFERENCE
Rain on the 1 California

"Out — coming out!"
"Back door!"
"How do you open these things?"
"Out!"

Every window steamed. From the back seats
we can't hear the driver. We count stops
to know where we are, sometimes get off
and are surprised.

We breathe air that hangs thick with wet wool,
sodden umbrellas, ripening fruit,
like a second grade classroom at rainy day lunch.

The bus brakes. Doors open. A heavy blue-eyed
blond pushes up the steps. She carries an infant,
two brimming tote bags, and four red carnations.
One arm slung around a pole, she shows us her
baby's face.

Everything changes.

PENTHOUSE
5 Jackson, Saturday Afternoon

Round and Russian, she
and her worn, thin husband
climb on board, her vehement speech
fountaining, filling aisles and ears
with unintelligible urgency.

The soft globe of her perfectly wound
and anchored topknot lurches and bobs
with the braking bus and her convictions.

What could be inside that quivering orb?
Extra cash? Emergency chocolate?
Easter eggs? Or a wondrous refuge
from a world without silence?

STOP REQUESTED

EROS BOUND/UNBOUND
Fields Bookstore

My chosen bookstore
where I go to browse
and buy, not expecting
to hear whispered
promises of conjunctio
from virginal volumes
hot off the press.

The pressure
of book with book
yields a secret sweat,
an erotic fragrance
enticing me
to sniff new pages,
stroke their terrains,
separate carefully
what has never before
been opened.

SLIGHTLY DAMAGED BUDDHAS
20% OFF

In silence, shopworn Siddhartha sits
on a shelf, eyes downcast, lips turning
toward a smile, revealing
how time and experience
can etch and scar wisdom's markings
into bronze or clay or human flesh.

EXCHANGE
The Asian Art Museum

I wander among
antique Japanese baskets.
Bamboo root handles twist and arc
above woven forms,
holding empty space,
holding all jewels,
holding me.

CAFÉ MUSEO
Museum of Modern Art

"Look!" he cries,
"Sunlight on the table leg."
Steel sends a luminous disc
to the cafe floor,
covering crumbs, scratches, faded stains.
The life-giving center of Earth's orbit
comes in silence, without appointment.

GEORGIA O'KEEFE
At the De Young

Black Cross and Red Sky
hangs glass-protected in a gallery,
as though the painting wore a veil,
as Moses did to protect the people
after communing with God.

Lights overhead reflect our faces,
pulling us into the painting,
its pigments darkening our features,
as if to let us glimpse the dying
required of living.

PEACEABLE KINGDOM
At the Corner of Geary and Laguna

Two stone lions guard the red entry
to the Chinese Consulate. Each
holds a small stone ball in its mouth,
rattling threats to evil spirits. If roused,
the cats will summon the mighty dragon
snaking through Chinatown
at New Year. No one dares
disturb these wild creatures, who sit
eternally cold and open-eyed
on the master's threshold.

Who was it, then, who placed
a clutch of spring flowers
in each leering mouth?

STEALING MARC CHAGALL

Museum of Modern Art

Lovers in Green,
Lovers in Gray,
Lovers Flying Above the Town.
Intimate love songs in oils,
windows open into hope.
Faces shine. Children point.
We are in a temple.

A great-bellied man ambles
across our vision, barely glancing
at paintings only inches
from the phone at his right ear.

He walks, talks, stops, eyes closed.
"How rude!" I cry, as though shot.
"How really rude!" I wail.
He slows down.
"How really really rude!"
I howl, to applause.

He stops, mutters
to an invisible other,
"It's awfully hard to talk in here."
He folds up the phone,
slips around a corner,
disappears.

We turn again to
Lovers in Green,
Lovers in Gray,
Lovers Flying Above the Town.
A cell phone rings in the next gallery.
The entire exhibit vanishes.

HIGH COST OF LIVING

"Do you work here?"
"Sure do —"
"I'm looking for a laptop."
 "I can help you,"

says a boy, round-faced,
twitching left eye. He tells me,
"I'm too smart for school —
love music, books.
I'm a fool who knows
I'm nothing."

We finish the sale. He asks,
"Do you play an instrument?"
"Piano."
"Thought so. You're the type. My Mom
played too."
"Does she still?"
"She's dead. A month ago. Shot herself.
I found her."

KANGA GOES TO THE GYM

Black mutt puppy,
front legs incomplete,
scoots to the gym,
rump high
over arched spine.
With persistent energy
she hops and pushes,
bearing her beauty
in the curve of her back.

SNAKE MAN'S GRANNY

Man with Snake Tattoos on Treadmill:

I used to weigh 350 pounds, with a 52 inch waist.
But I lost it. How? Changed my way of life. That's how.
Not a diet. Way of life. Health is what I live for.
Don't want anything else. Nothing's more important.
My grandma's nearly eighty. She's had two face lifts,
her breasts fixed, and a tummy tuck. Walks a good
six miles on a treadmill every day. Does she look fabulous!

Dour Man on Treadmill:

My granny was a mean old drunk.

Woman with Peace T-shirt on Treadmill:

Mine was a Methodist,
took the Women's Temperance Union
pledge, never touched a drop, never
went to a gym, never failed to look
every minute of her age.
She watched birds every day, stars every night,
studied the burrs she took from our sweaters,
led swarming bees out of our house
with a handkerchief. She studied medicine,
loved to shop, hated to cook, dreamed
of singing. She knew poverty and plenty.
She was too quiet.
I wish I'd asked her questions.

A CONCERT TALE
for Elizabeth Blumenstock

She comes onstage to play Vivaldi,
tunes her violin,
draws a bow over the first bars.

Primavera comes alive —
mountain spring waters ooze
and splash from every note,
until

the music stops.

Dangling from her bow:
a tuft of tail from the donor horse.
The hairs sway as they once did
in summer rains, switch back
and forth, as though remembering
how they could scatter fifty flies
with one flick.

New bow in hand,
she tosses her mane,
nods to all present,
begins again.

JESSYE NORMAN

Davies Symphony Hall

Twenty feet tall,
robed like a queen
in satin and hair –
magical tresses,
spinning and black.
They grow as she sings,
entangle Row A,
wind all of us tight
take us her prisoners
carry us with her
into the night.

EAST BROTHER ISLAND
San Francisco Bay

East Brother Island grew a lighthouse
like a lone tree.
Its beaconed crown sweeps a rim
of horizon, circling
without end, by midnight,
by noon. I climb its trunk
on spiral stairs. The turning lamp
at the center lights the passage
of my live and turning body.

CATHEDRAL BELLS
St. Mary's on Cathedral Hill

Ave, Ave, Ave Maria,
ringing the hours
morning to evening,
ringing to all.

Ave,
homeless man, back against
a mail box, reading A Brief History
of Everything from a stack of books.

Ave,
old man selling Street Sheet
for a dollar, pointing to his poem
on page seven, asking if we want two copies.

Ave,
little girl in long pink pinafore,
pirouetting to the ballet
applauded by her Mama.

Ave,
government clerk putting on a raincoat
blowing his own storm
into a large, crumpled handkerchief.

Ave,
at noon, Ave at six,
bells for the Angelus,
Gabriel telling impossible birth.

Ave,
tolling for death, a single slow bell,
ring, ring, ring, ring,
one day for us, one day for us.

Ave, Ave, Ave Maria,
ring us alive,
ring what you know.

JUBILATE
Grace Cathedral

Singing plays a cathedral
like a rare violin. Voices
waken sleeping echoes,
spiral through arches,
tickle the vaulted ceiling,
sending the Virgin's foot
tapping, the Child's rattle
shaking, calling saints
from their niches to twirl
through the transept, throwing
coins and confetti
to the devout in their pews,
bringing glee to the gargoyles
who leer in exultation,
rousing the Holy Spirit
from above the high altar,
to visit everyone present
and tend the small flame
that burns without fail
in the ear of the heart.

PLEASE HOLD ON

DARK BEAUTY

I live in a city,
beautiful among cities,
petaled and perfumed
with voluptuous spring.
I pause before a cherry tree's
extravagance,
losing myself in sunlight
through petals.
A man curls at the roots,
wrapped in a quilt,
himself once the bud
of a child.

NEW WHITE CANE

I carry it clumsily, wanting to be brave.
Waiting on the corner of Fillmore and Pine
for a green light, two young women talk
as they lean against a lamp post:
"That mother fuckin' asshole prick couldn't ..."
They look at me, stop. One calls,
"The light is with you, dear — the light is with
you." I feel a blessing spill over me
like spring sun, warming the January chill.
"Thanks!" The red flashes. "OK, dear —"
she says, turning to her friend, "He couldn't even aim his
    piss" — the light turns. Our lives go on.

WIND PLAY

I step into June
light and shadow,
spy a cellophane wrapper
rolling fast on west wind.
Flashes of sun ripple and dart,
the clear husk loops and skips,
the heavenly fire's
newest toy.

WHAT LEAPS IN US

I pass by a city fountain,
see strangers gazing
into flowering spray.
I feel the exuberant spring
at the center,
and the mist
of its sunlit arc
flung into the sky
from which it falls,
to which it returns.

A LEASH A KITE STRING

Once I knew a grass-clothed hill
wearing radish, dock and rattlesnake weed.
Each year with friends I'd climb its sunny crown
with kites and champagne
to hold the sky in place with airborne sails
of silken birds, moons and ribboned fish.

I'd unwind my string, let it go taut,
remember death, and dream awake
of gliding and tumbling unstrung.

Now I walk a city's hills
with a dog named Joy.
Her leash tugs like a kite string, pulling me
to stones, roots, clay and concrete.
I hold a line to the taste of wind,
to the sight of how the body speaks,
to the sounds of birds weaving nests
and snails traveling slow,
to what paws read as they sniff new trails.

The live sky of that long ago hill has fallen
to earth and shines through.

FLOWERING ROSHI
At Ellis and Gough

The pregnant woman touches
her shining world-belly
with anxious prayer.
The sleeper wakes in dread,
counts breath, names bones,
as hours creep sideways.
Sounds of killing
streak through day
and the heart gives its treasure
to barring the door.

In such a time,
plum trees do not forget
to flower first, opening
mid-winter petals
to brief sun,
letting white skins
and red centers catch
rain, the robin's eye,
the gaze of strangers,
who stop each other
on a city street to wonder,
    "How long will they last?"
"Maybe a week."
"So fragile."
They walk on,
their bond the surprise of rebirth.

UNHOLY SAMARITAN

A man lies alone in the blinking
of a grocery store beer sign,
his body folded in a fetal bundle,
as though he were a womb for himself
this January night. Alone.
Uncovered legs twitch.
Too little clothing.
Drenched with damp.

I pass by.

FILLMORE STREET FAIR

Near the "Local Cheese" table
sits a woman on in years
and in her cups.
Her gray hair hangs
like bearded moss on a live oak.
Though her eyes are open,
their shades are drawn.
Spine curled forward,
she seems unaware
of fists spilling with cash,
held on her knees.
Vulnerable, exposed,
surrounded by empty beer cans
and Independence Day revelers,
she is a silent child with secret loss.

SHE SAYS HER NAME IS SHERRY

Cross-legged on quilts, Sherry leans
her generous back against a street lamp,
rocks two giant teddy bears, bends over them,
swaying. Strands of gray-blond hair
stroke their stained fur. A cellist
from nearby Symphony Hall greets her,
folds a dollar into a worn paper cup,
stays to chat. She looks up,
tries to focus, nose and cheeks ripening.
"Thank you, darlin'. God bless — you hear?"
He doesn't move on. She adds,
"Wanna see somethin' neat? Got me a kitten.
Name's Nettie." She lifts a ripped blanket.
A small soft body wakens in its nest.
He steps back, pulls out a kleenex. "Cat allergy.
Just the sight of them —." Sherry nods.
"I know, honey. We all have something that's tough."

AFTER CHRISTMAS

Corpses of cedars and firs
poke through body bags
at the curb. Tinsel
clings to their necks.
Faux snow sparkles
on their limbs.

Night wind sings carols.
Dry needles break,
sending ornament shards
to the sidewalk, pieces of memory
waiting for tomorrow's broom.

Holiday lights gone dark,
hide coals in the heart.

AFTER NIGHT RAIN

Puddle.
Window at your feet.
Look through:
a star sees you.
Flags fly upside down.
City Hall's gold cupola
quivers on its head,
shaking its luminous spire
off-balance,
ready to topple
into night sky.

LEFT BEHIND

The senior class has gone
into the wilderness
of dissonance and dream.

Scattered in front of the school
lie empty shoes and sweats,
as on a beach at low tide.

What happened here, in the midst of
Pomp and Circumstance? Abduction by aliens?
The Rapture? Some taken into Paradise, some
left to live here below? Taken right out
of their shoes and everything else. Taken into
more of graduation than they ever imagined.

Bless the bodies that lived in these garments.
May they be wrapped in mercy and hope
as they take their turn at evolution's tip.

PROPHETS

Pages of today's Chronicle
hobble down the sidewalk
like wings without birds to fly them.
Their corners catch a wind gust
sending headlines airborne:

 Shaky Cease-fire
 Falling Purse Power
Record Lotto
  Small Nukes Next?
  Ten Day Bali Getaway

Crackling, scraping, folded wings
of a day's news
swoop and slide, their messages
torn and stained.
We walk blind upon their warnings.

JAZZ IN THE MORNING

Through an open car window,
music — soul seed
scattered over paved city land.
Cracks and grates furrow
dampened streets, ready
for planting saxophone solos
and keyboard melismas.
Who will tend this garden?

LISTEN

You come singing, opera student,
climbing Scott Street, notes flying free
from your mouth, taking wing
toward Monterey Pines in Alta Plaza Park.

You are contagious.
I sing, too,
finding in you
my own music.

SUMMER FOG

Touching my cheek
with the back of its long
cool hand, touching
without need for name,
as though it were kin.

I press into this cloud,
letting what is clear, familiar,
fall away.

FIRE AND WATER

Fog wings fold, unfold,
weave a wreath for City Hall's
gold cupola, veil its glow,
as though for a bride.

Sun barely brightens high noon,
silvering cloud edges.
The sun-starved among us
catch a solar truffle, small and sweet.

STUDENTS OF THE SEA

Tourists wear t-shirts and shorts
in the morning. By three o'clock,
they've bought sweaters. Every year,
unsuspecting newcomers

are swept out to sea at Ocean Beach,
where rip current and undertow pull
under pacific surface. Waders are taken
into what they have not chosen.

Always changing, always the same,
the sea lets us make our own mistakes,
erodes illusions of control,
punishes ignorance of the deep.

WHAT SOLES KNOW

I walk city sidewalks, on a buried past
of teeth, tools, beads, shells,
pots, hides, knives, rings.
Shards of life before —
before the cart without horses,
the ship with wings,
and the luminous tear drop
of the light bulb.

Bones of the dead drum us alive.
We hear them beating in our blood,
pulsing as we step step step
on the ground where they made fire
in the night, made love, made war,
danced in ceremony,
danced in celebration.

We cover the past with concrete
and cultivation. We plant gardens
upon it, fix our foundations,
travel aware and unaware
over its pain and its meaning.

The past accompanies us, tells
what it knows through our footprints.
What difference will it make?

THANK YOU FOR RIDING MUNI

SAN FRANCISCO IRISH BLESSING

May the road that rises steeply before you
    not drop you over a cliff on the other side,
May the wind at your back be free of dust
    and diesel fumes,
May the green lights wait long for your sweet appearing,
May the MUNI hold its doors open for your boarding,
    the riders cheer, and offer you seats,
May the great flocks of God's good pigeons
    shit anywhere but on your head,
May all who drive the cars, trucks and busses
    round about you greet you with gracious smiles,
May your pockets be ever filled with exact change
    for public transport and parking meters,
May parking places open before you, behind you,
    to the right and to the left of you,
May the movie or the concert never start without you,
May homeless men and women find food and shelter
    for the night, and in the morning, work
      that pays a living wage,
May the geometry of one-way streets never confuse you,
May God gentle the sound of the jack-hammer, leaf blower,
    and car alarm,
May you avoid stepping into any manhole left uncovered,
May your house be always filled with flowers,
And may the years to come be graced with true friends,
    who will travel with you through all the nights and days
    of your blessed life.

Meeting Your City

MEETING YOUR CITY

San Francisco beckons. It wants participants, wants to be experienced. Here are some ways to begin. One of these ideas might tickle your curiosity, elbow your imagination. Experiment.

Expedition

Enter the city as you would wilderness country, as an unknown place, needing openness and respect. Chart its territory. Make your own map. Who lives here? What grows in its earth? Take field notes.

Vision Quest

With a question or concern in your pocket, walk through the city, noticing what crosses your path, what lodges in you. Let yourself be surprised. Be aware of what you overhear. Notice a fragrance that may stir memory. Pay attention to details that strike you as odd, lovely, or amusing. Who turns your head twice? Whatever happens, ponder how it speaks to the question or concern you bring with you on this walk.

Interconnection

Find a place where you can watch a variety of people come and go: a café, the Greyhound Bus Depot, or Union Square. Imagine a thread connecting you with someone who catches your attention. Thread yourself to another person – and another.

The Camera's Eye

Take a camera into the city. What moments does it want to remember? What poems and stories do they tell you? What has stayed with you, when you look at the pictures later?

Muni Marathon

Ride, ride, ride, especially the long lines that travel through several neighborhoods, like the 38 Geary, 19 Polk, 30 Stockton, 22 Fillmore, 24 Divisadero, and 1 California. Observe these neighborhoods, and the people who get on and off.

Homeless People

Look into their eyes. Buy and read Street Sheet. Talk with them, if both of you agree. What stories do they tell? Where do they eat, find shelter, get medical help?

Treasure Hunt

Search for beauty. It shows up in the least likely places. Peer down alleys, into office windows, through gates. Check out Laundromats, cafe bulletin boards, schoolyards, BART stations, gutters, pigeons. Look at human faces, animals, architecture, reflected light and shadow, patterns in cracks, spots and trash, the textures of things.

Be A Building

Go into different kinds of buildings. Each has a personality and a history. Imagine yourself as one of them. Are you friendly to other buildings? Do you block views? Are people happy in and around you? What goes on inside? Do birds like you? Can you breathe? Do you get enough sunshine? Do trees and flowers do well near you? Is there anything that needs repair and remodeling?

Choreography

The city dances. Follow its movement patterns, its paces, rhythms, uses of space. How do urban folk move? Where is the stillness? What music would you use for these movements?

City Stories

Imagine what you are seeing as a movie or a play. Everywhere you look, a story is unfolding. How would you tell them? For example, what story might be happening were you to observe the following:

- A white-robed man in his thirties eats alone and writes with a fountain pen in a big book.
- One woman says to another, "After forty years, she saw him on a BART train, going the other way!"
- An ambulance, siren wailing, roars through an intersection.
- An old man sleeps in a large cardboard box.
- A woman's expensive high-heeled shoe lies on a park bench.

At the opera house, a young woman, wearing a long green satin gown, sits at a table with a young man, wearing a tuxedo. They drink red wine and eat gummy bears.

Found Poems

Write a poem, using only words and phrases from store names, street signs, theater marquis, headlines, billboards, bumper stickers, flyers taped to poles and graffiti.

Soundings

Stand out of doors in the city. Close your eyes. What do you hear – far away, nearby, inside your body? Walk through city streets. What do you hear that is jazzy, lyrical, booming, drumming, tinkling, strident? Where is the singing? Where are the bells? Where is the silence and what is the sound of it?

Tracking

If you had just arrived in San Francisco from another planet, what would you make of the tracks at your feet? Study the paw prints, footprints, bird tracks, tire tracks, and all the spots and dabs from living beings in motion.

Portraits

Write or sketch portraits of people you observe in the city. What can you tell about them by their body language, clothing, what they carry, what they do and do not say?

Other Shoes

Imagine you are a sea gull, a guide dog, the Mayor, a homeless person, a waitress, a stray cat, a financier, a well-kept poodle, a bus driver, a public school seventh grader. What would it be like to experience the world from this other's experience and perspective?

Trash

Who and what are discarded in the city? What value might they have? Marginalized people can be among the most generous, compassionate and intriguing. Junkyard throwaways can fuel a sculptor's vision. Thrift shops and garage sales can offer treasures.

The City's Past

As you wander through city streets, imagine who walked there before you and what the land was like when there were no streets. What lies buried beneath your feet?

Unlikely Dialogues

As you travel the city, imagine conversations between strange partners, such as:

- An earthquake and a skyscraper
- A cable car and the steepest hill on its route
- A six-year-old child in the Tenderloin and the principal of an exclusive private elementary school
- A corporate executive and a musician playing for pennies in a BART station
- The Palace Hotel and City Lights Book Store
- The clock on the Ferry Building and yesterday's newspaper scuttling down Market Street

Murals

Look for murals throughout the city – inside Coit Tower, the Rincon Annex Post office, on walls south of Market, and in the Mission District. What do they tell you? What other spaces need murals? What would you paint there?

Water

Make a pilgrimage to seven of the city's fountains. Find a favorite and have a picnic. Visit the beaches. Walk along the Crissy Field path to the Golden Gate Bridge. Visit the Wave Organ. Go to the top of the Fillmore Street Steps, and sit awhile, looking out over the Marina and the bay to the Marin Headlands.

The Creative Core

For many people, the city inspires creativity. Where do you find it in San Francisco? The daily paper lists mainstream and experimental offerings, though you may come upon the unlisted – the street artists and performers, the jugglers, fire-eaters and people who make gravity-defying rock piles by the bay.

Leaving In – Leaving Out

Many of us experience an unfamiliar place through the lenses of what is familiar. Sometimes we need to shake ourselves into asking what we are leaving out, so that we look for what we haven't seen, listen to what we haven't heard, and open all of our senses to what is foreign to us.

Bridging

Cross San Francisco's bridges. Walk. Ride. Stand mid-span on the Golden Gate Bridge. Look at the city from this place of in-between. Stretch out your arms toward one side and the other, embracing the whole of the city, the whole of yourself.